I ♥ My Hair

very Dirty Blonde

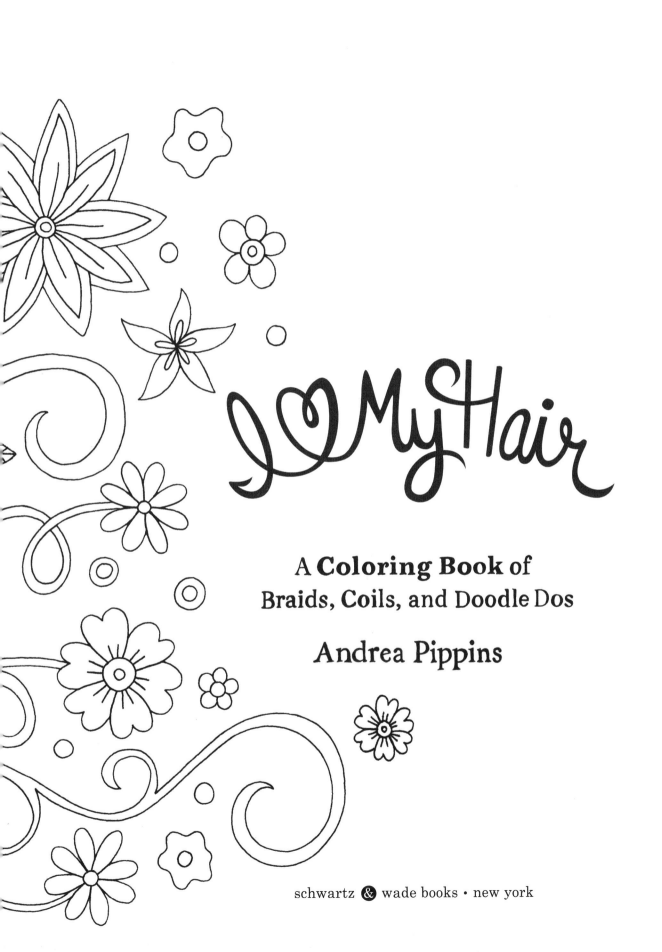

I ♥ My Hair

A **Coloring Book** of
Braids, Coils, and Doodle Dos

Andrea Pippins

schwartz & wade books · new york

**For my parents, Regina and James,
who always encouraged me to follow my dreams**

All rights reserved. Published in the United States by Schwartz & Wade Books, an imprint of Random House Children's Books, a division of Penguin Random House LLC, New York.

Schwartz & Wade Books and the colophon are trademarks of Penguin Random House LLC.

Visit us on the Web! randomhouseteens.com

The illustrations in this book were rendered in Sakura Pigma Micron pens.
Book design by Rachael Cole

ISBN 978-0-399-55122-2

Printed in the United States of America
2 4 6 8 10 9 7 5 3 1
First Edition

This book
belongs to

Wesley B.T.

Like a lot of women, I have worn my hair many different ways over the years—close-cropped and long, straightened and natural, pulled into tight cornrows or let loose into a big bouncy 'fro.

As an artist and a designer, I'm all about self-empowerment for women and girls, and much of my artwork over the years has been inspired by social, political, and cultural statements that can be made with hair. I first started creating art prints celebrating hair in 2008 for my thesis project in grad school, which was a campaign to encourage African American women to love and embrace their naturally coily hair. Little did I know that this would lead me to the very book you're holding.

Inside this book, you'll find pages filled with doodles that continue to celebrate my love for black hair, and my passion for inspiring all women and girls to feel good about themselves.

You can color in the pages using artist's-quality colored pencils, which are good for blending and shading, or fine-tipped pens for vibrant blocks of color. And feel free to add your own doodles to any page. To embellish or extend a drawing, use a fine-tipped black pen—I like Sakura Pigma Micron pens, which I used to create the art in this book.

Happy coloring,

Andrea Pippins
♡ ☺

Be You

My hair is...

Cute

HOT

BOLD

FUNKY

FLY

superb

POWERFUL

BIG

happy

CLASSIC

FABULOUS

pretty

COOL

GORGEOUS

DOPE

SOPHISTICATED

SOFT

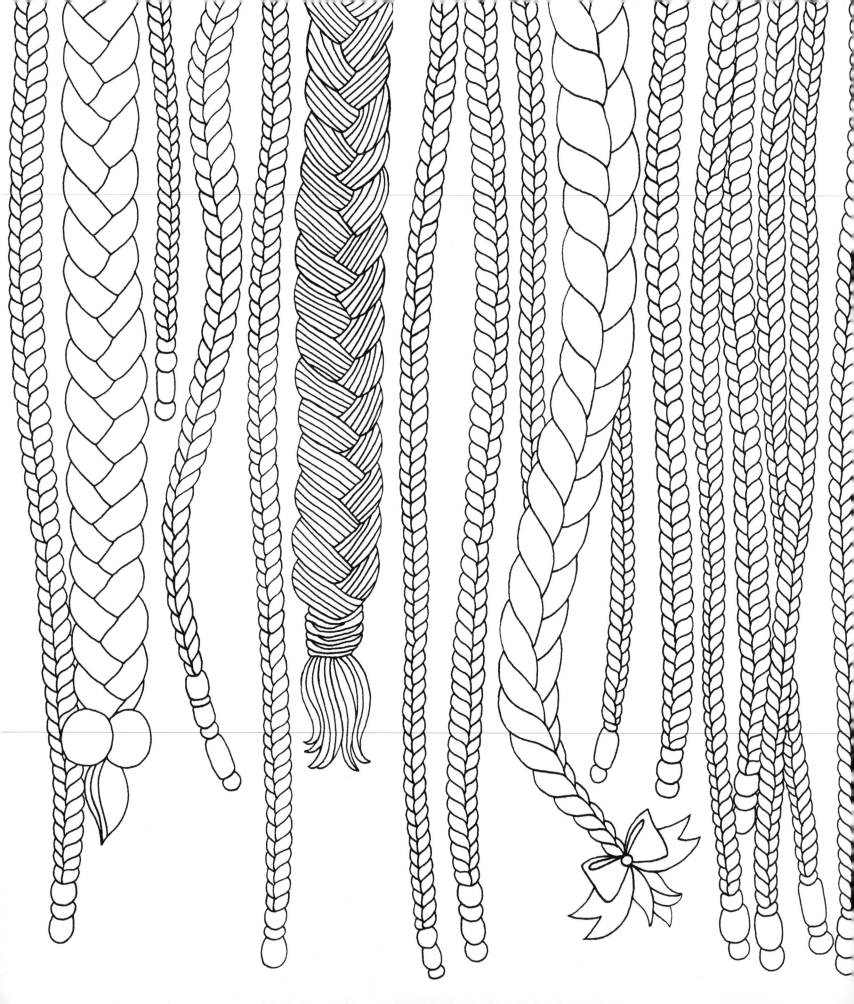

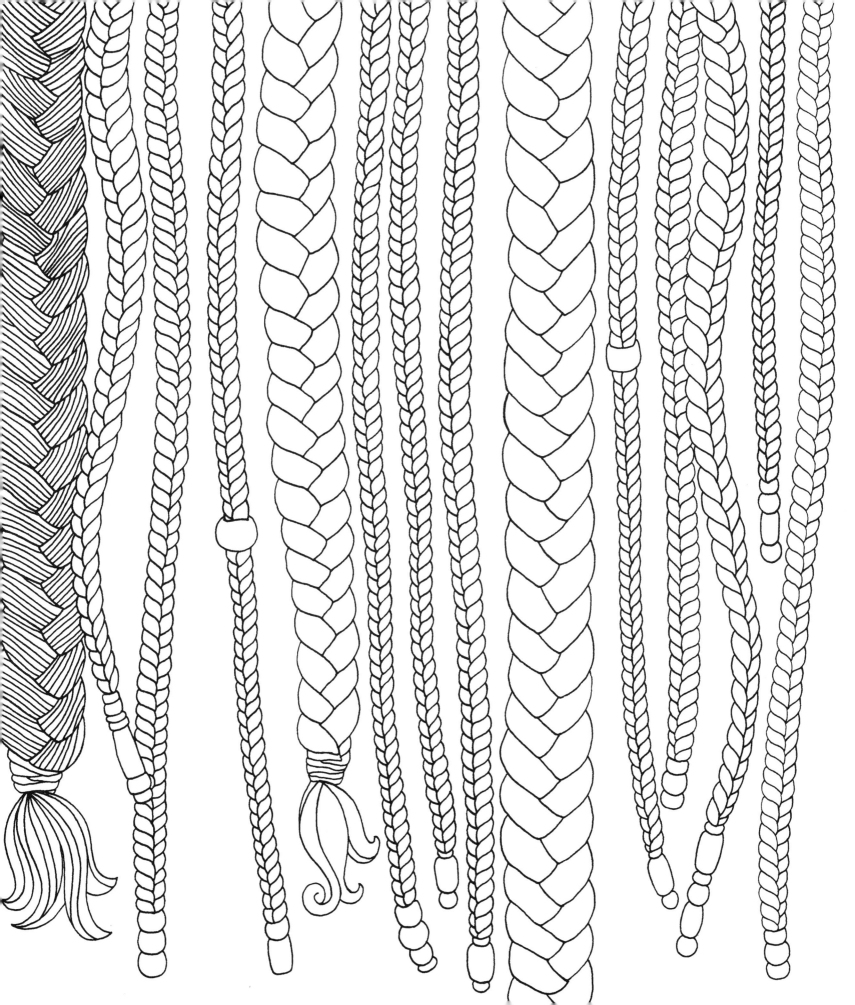

Go cropped & coily

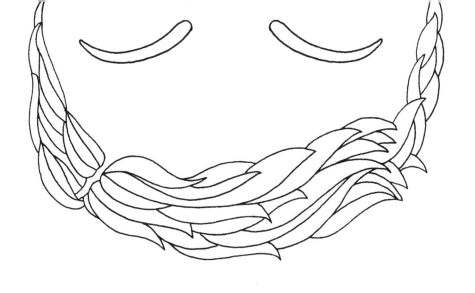

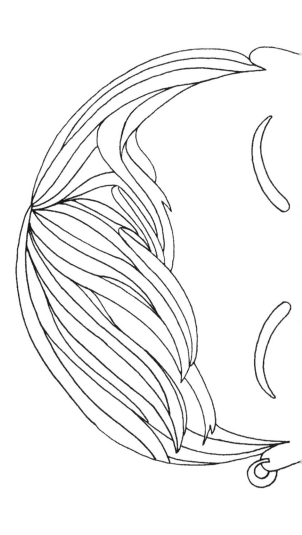

or SHORT & SPiKY

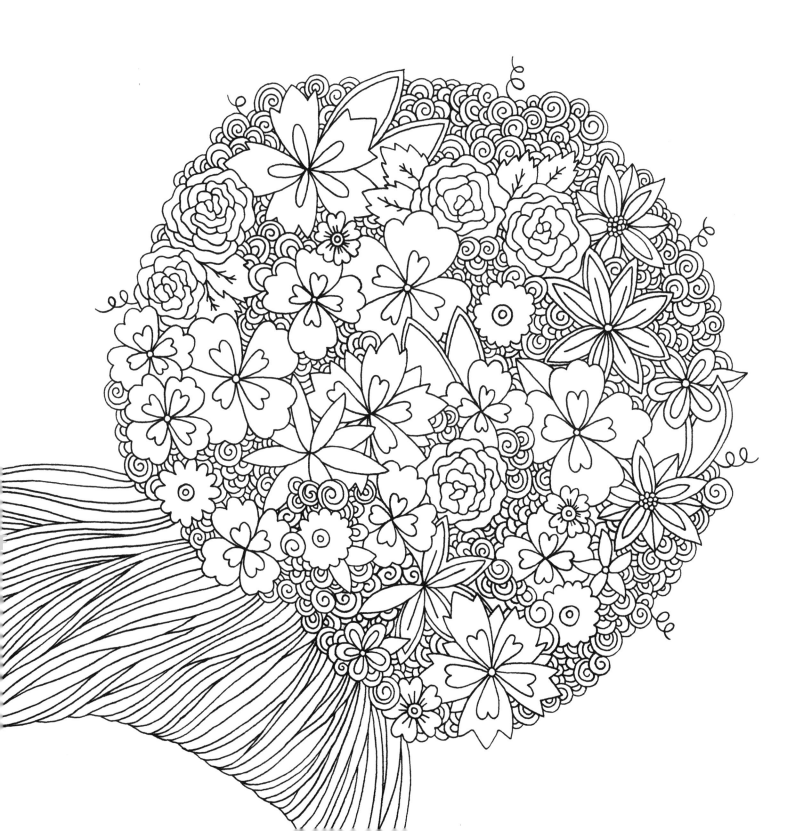

WASH
CURL
TRIM
CUT
LOCK
FLAT-IRON
CONDITION
GREASE
SPRAY
PINNED UP
BRUSH
STYLE
RINSE

South Indian
BEJEWELED BRIDAL BRAID

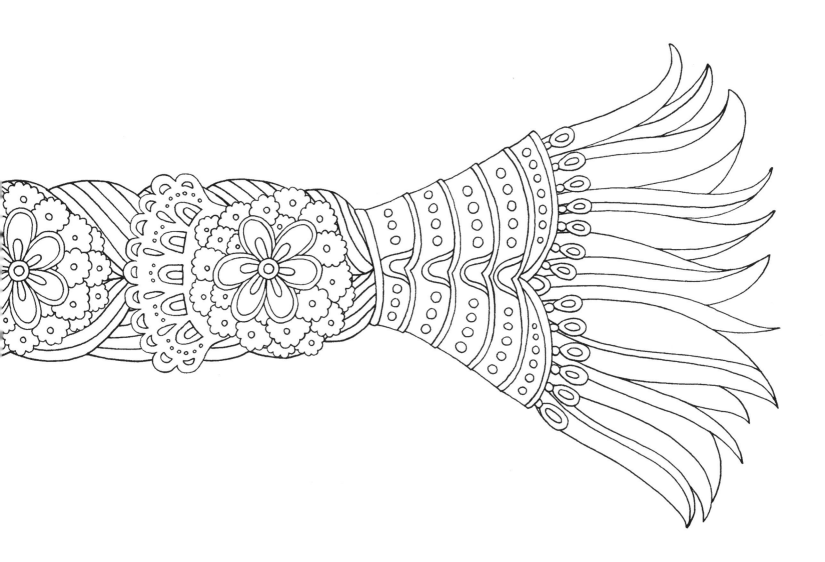

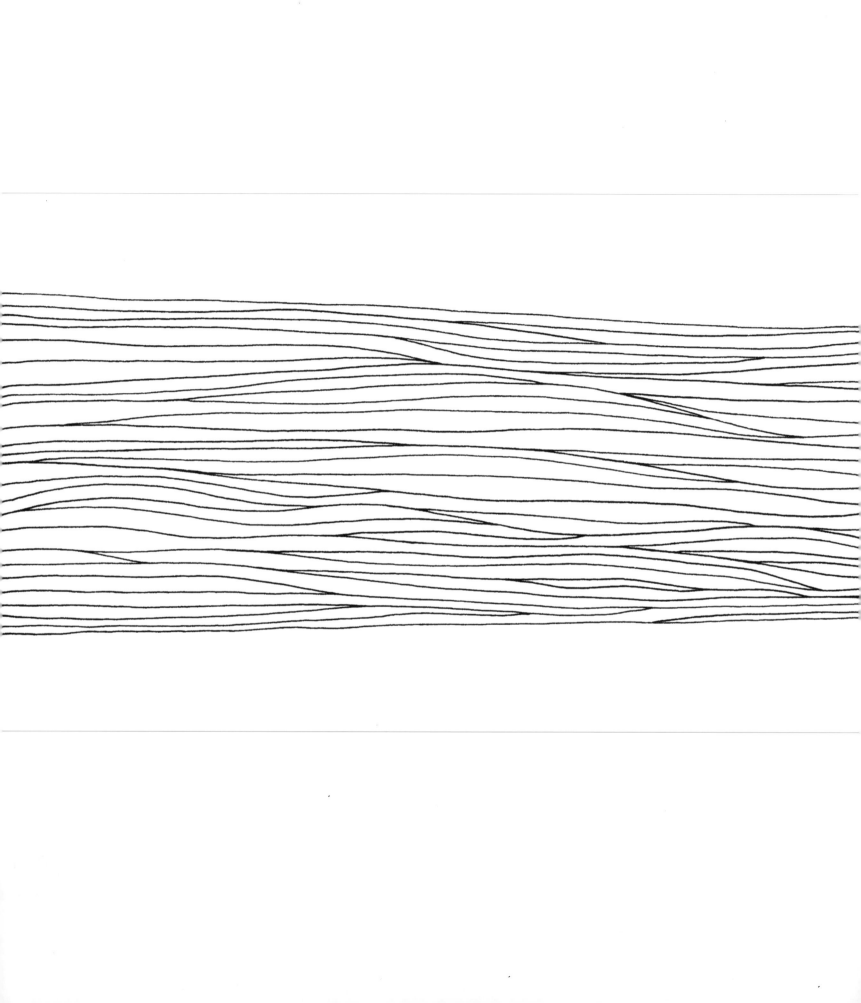

Carmen Miranda

CROWNS for

YOUR CROWN

ADORN LIKE an EGYPTIAN Queen

MAMI WATA

relax & LET YOUR hair GO free

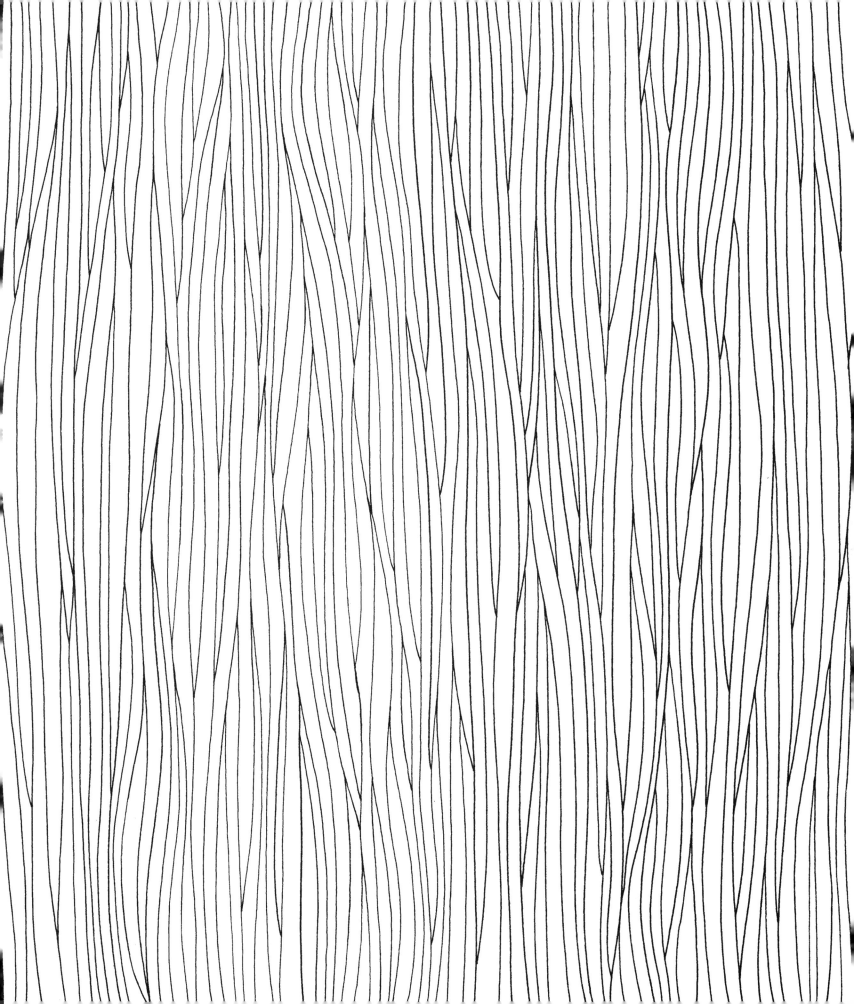

BOXBRAIDS • UPDO

twists • AFRO

pageboy • gumby

finger • CORNROWS

waves • SHAG BO

BEEHIVE

PONYTAIL

DREAD

bouffant

LOCKS

PIXIE CUT

BUN

J'heri

top knot

French BRAID

curl

CHIGNON

HI-TOP FADE ↑

mohawk

MY HAIR

a BIG THANK YOU

To my mom and dad, Rachael Cole, Lee Wade, Cassie McGinty, Stephanie Pitts, Kelly Holohan, Danielle Finney, Shadra Strickland, and Kiona Graham. To all the friends who called to check up on me on a regular basis during the entire drawing process. And a huge hug to all the I Love My Hair friends who have supported my artwork over the years. Thank you. You all are a part of my dream.

Particularly proud of a piece? We would love to see your creations, which, like your own beautiful hair, will be unique to you. On social media, please use the hashtags #IHeartMyHair and #andreapippins so we'll be sure to see your posts.